Sticks Stones and Stumped!

Deb Landry

An educational interactive children's play on bullying and harassment prevention

Teacher's Guide, Scripts & Student Workbook
ISBN number 978-0-9773738-2-6
Library of Congress 2008909424

Cover design by Donna Berger
Book Illustrated by Melissa Pelletier
Set design by Amy Cote

Sticks Stones and Stumped is the proud recipient of the
2007 Family Review Center Gold Award

Play Rights © Sticks Stones and Stumped! Written by Deb Landry, Bryson Taylor Publishing, 199 New County Road, Saco ME 04072 Copyright 2007 License information available by contacting www.brysontaylorpublishing.com All rights reserved. No part of this publication may be reproduced or transmitted in any form or by any means, electronic or mechanical, including photocopy, recording, or any information storage and retrieval system, without the express written authorization of the author. Licensee may not change any part of the story without permission. Billing of the author must follow the title on any and all publicity. Author's bio must be printed in any program. Author has the right to attend one performance free of charge. Billing of the author must follow the title on any and all publicity. A bio downloadable is available on the website. Rights to this play are available for one year at which time a $50 fee is due each year you wish to perform this play past that one-year time if admission is charged.

Sticks and Stones

Sticks and stones may break my bones,
But names will never hurt me.
And this I knew was always true
And truth would not desert me.
But now I know it is not so,
I've learned the other part;
For sticks and stones may break the bones,
But words can break the heart.
Yes, sticks and stones may break the bones
And leave the spirit whole;
But unkind words can break the spirit,
And silently crush the soul.

~~ Author Unknown ~~

Chapman, what is bullying?

Well Felicia, I looked it up in the dictionary and it says that it is mean, cruel or overbearing abusive behavior. Bullying is also when someone is treated in a harassing or intimidating manner. It's a behavior that can be aggressive and happens in a mean way through words and actions.

Contents

	Page
Introduction	I
Scene 1	1
Scene 2	2
Scene 3	5
Scene 4	7
Scene 5	9
Scene 6	10
Scene 7	12
Production Note Page	18
Classroom Preparation	19
Classroom Expectations	20
Classroom Discussion	21
Costumes and Props	23
Production Tips	24
Scenery Examples	25
Teacher to Parent Communication	26

Workbook Pages begin at Page 29
- School poster
- Bookmark
- STANDbyer Fallen Phrases
- Bully Facts & Sticks, Stones and Stumpers!
- The Apple Tree Exercise
- Classic Stumper Word Find
- Special Message Scrambler
- Possum Facts
- Take home booklet two pages
- Certificate of Completion
- Cut and Copy Student Script

Some color downloads are available at www.brysontaylorpublishing.com) or by emailing info@brysontaylorpublishing.com

Introduction

Sticks Stones and Stumped the play is intended to raise awareness of bullying and harassment prevention in schools and youth programming. The interactive play and book is designed as a learning tool to cultivate an environment where children can openly discuss sensitive issues whether they are the targeted victim, bystander or bully. By using the characters in this story rather than actual situations, students can role-play and express their feelings in a safe and non-threatening environment.

Research indicates that youth involved in the arts do better in school, are more involved in their communities and demonstrate better attitudes toward themselves and others. Results also show an increased ability to express anger appropriately and to communicate effectively with both peers and adult, ultimately developing the skills to make healthy, safe choices. Therefore, interactive play strengthens relationships, increases awareness and assist in understanding social behaviors, which directly results in a reduction of bullying, intimidation, exclusion and harassment.

In order for this or any program to be effective, it is imperative for the schools, afterschool programs, classroom and staff to adopt a policy that is adapted from a comprehensive researched based anti bullying and harassment program. Educating and empowering bystanders, supportive school administration, parents and adult support (safe places and caring adults) are the key factors in creating an atmosphere where children can feel safe and learn. Most States have laws. A quick and up to date means to view State laws is at www.bullypolice.com.

For the best results, use this awareness based play as a group project. Employ parent volunteers in making costumes, building props and painting the scenery. Building connections and teams make theater projects a memorable experience for parents, teachers, program directors and especially the youth and children. Other suggested productions are classroom reader's theater, peer performances, and mentoring performances using either upper classmates or teachers.

Sticks, Stones and Stumped!

Interactive Children's Bullying and Harassment Prevention Play

By Deb Landry

Scene 1

Description: Billy Bob Opossum has migrated to Maine from the south. He is excited about his first day at school and meeting his new teacher and classmates.

Place: In the kitchen of Billy Bob's new tree house.

Mama O
(*Mama O speaks with a southern accent. She wears an apron, which can have a couple of stuffed opossums sticking out of the pockets. She is cleaning up around the kitchen, looks around and doesn't see Billy Bob*) Billy Bob, it's time to get ready for school. Don't forget to brush your teeth and make your bed.

Billy Bob
(*Jumps up from behind the stage, fully dress and taps Mama on the shoulder, he speaks in a southern accent, smiles to show his clean teeth*) Here I am Mama O. I'm all ready for school and have all my chores done! I'm so excited I just couldn't sleep any longer.

Mama O
Oh, Billy Bob you look so handsome! Do you have your lunch and your… (*Billy interrupts*).

Billy Bob
Mama I have everything. (*Patting his pouch, Billy has on a baseball hat; he does not carry a backpack*) I'm going to walk with Chapman. He said he would introduce me to his friends and we would have so much fun, especially at recess time and playing stickball.

(*There is a knock on the door.*)*Billy goes to answer the door, hurrying with excitement.*)

Billy Bob
Hey, Chapman

Chapman
Hey Billy Bob, Mrs. O, are you ready to go?

Billy Bob
Ya! I can't wait, let's get going.
(*They run off stage. Mama smiles at the boys and waves goodbye.*)

Scene 2

Place: Inside the classroom of Miss Dorrie Deer. Scenery can be inside of a tree with stumps as desks. See samples of scenery on page 17. Cubby Bear and Felicia Fox enter and sit on their stumps making small talk. Billy Bob and Chapman then enter and Billy is introduced to Felicia Fox, Cubby Bear, and the rest of the class, which is the audience. (Bull E Moose, can be seated in the audience, eavesdrops on the conversation by making an earlier entrance before the show or he can make a grand entrance later). Billy and Chapman are standing, Felicia and Cubby stand up to be introduced, draws attention to them. If Bull E is in the audience, he should ask the children to be quiet so he can hear what is going on.

Chapman
Billy Bob, these are my friends Felicia and Cubby. They play on my stickball team the Critters.

Felicia
Hi Billy Bob, welcome to *"Your School". (Insert your school name.)*

Cubby
Hey Billy Bob, Knock, Knock,

Billy Bob
Who's there?

Cubby
Spell

Billy Bob
Spell Who?

Cubby
W-H-O! *(They all laugh)*

Billy Bob
It's very nice to meet ya'll. *(Billy is chuckling; Felicia and Cubby sit back down in front of Bull E. Billy and Chapman sit in the front of the class on their stumps.)*

Felicia
Hey, Billy and Chapman, want to play with us at recess time? *(They nod yes with excitement.)*

Miss Dorrie Deer

Children, children, (*interrupting the conversation* and *ringing a bell, Miss Dorrie Deer comes in behind the audience or walking in from outside the classroom*) please stop talking and get to your seat, we need to get started. *(Children respond to the bell and begin to find a place to sit; the children in the audience are also included as they are part of the classroom. Dorrie walks through the audience checking to see that all children are quiet, listening and ready to learn, she talks to the children with a kind voice. She begins the dialog when she is in front of the class.)* Thank you very much children, it is so nice to see all of you after the long winter hibernation break. Welcome back! Before we get started with our class, I would like to introduce our new student, Billy Bob Opossum. *(Motions for Billy Bob to stand and children clap and yell from the audience. Felicia, Cubby and Chapman should start the applause, giving the other children permission to clap also, Bull E moves closer and joins the set)* Billy Bob, tell us a little about yourself and where you lived before you came to Maine.

Billy Bob

(Smiling shyly) Well Miss Dear, our family migrated here from Oklahoma. *(He continues to talk but can't be heard by anyone because Bull E is talking. Dorrie and Chapman, Felicia and Cubby listen, smiling with interest and shaking their heads to what Billy is saying, they cannot hear what Bull E. is saying to the audience)*

Bull E Moose

Well maybe he should go back "homa". What a weirdo, what kind of animal is he anyway? He's really ugly, and listen to the way he talks! *(Felicia gasps and looks disgusted at Bull E., scene goes back to Billy.)*

Billy Bob

....and I like to play stickball, do magic and collect odds and ends to store here in my pouch. Back home I was the catcher *(pulling out his stone ball out of his pouch)* on the Oakies and made 10 home runs last year! *(Billy Bob continues to talk but can't be heard)*

Bull E Moose

Big deal what a bragger, he's probably making up stories. Ten homeruns! Sure. And what's up with that pouch, I've never seen anything like that, I can imagine what else he keeps in there. What a flea infested nuisance.

Felicia

Stop it Bull E. It's not nice to say things like that. You don't want to hurt his feelings, do you? You know Billy Bob is harmless and seems like a very friendly guy.

Bull E Moose

Well, he's making up all these stories, I know he is.

Felicia
How do you know that? Anyway, we can always use another catcher and base runner for our team.

Cubby
Hey, I'm all for someone running the bases for me!

Bull E Moose
Not if I have anything to say about it. We're fine just the way we are. He can sit on the stump and keep score with *Chubby*. Better yet, he doesn't need to come at all.

Miss Dorrie Deer
Thank you, Billy Bob; we are very happy to have you here, right boys and girls?

Everyone except Bull E Moose
Yeah! *(Everyone claps)*

Miss Dorrie Deer
I hope you will like your new school and friends. Let me know if you need help. *(Billy sits down)* Okay children, today at recess we will have the tryouts for the spring stickball team. Anyone that is interested in playing on the Critter Team, meet me at the Pine Tree clearing field after school. Billy, I hope you will join the team! *(Billy and Chapman look at each other, shake their heads yes and smile excitedly)*

Bull E Moose
(Bragging) Well I guess we know who's going to be the star pitcher again this year! *(Looking around the room at everyone)* Don't bother trying out boys and girls, I've got this all wrapped up. *(Classmates look at each other puzzled).*

Miss Dorrie Deer
Okay children let's take out our nature book and get ready for our tree identification quiz! *(All the students respond with an: oh no.)*

Scene 3

In between scenes, Cubby Bear brings out a sign that says, **Later that afternoon.** *He can have it upside down or side ways, something to make the kids laugh. Place: Pine Tree Park. Bull E is tossing the ball by himself center stage, taking up a lot of space, showing off. The other characters are around the stage in various places.*

Billy Bob
Hey Chapman, want to see a magic trick? *(Billy pulls out some cards from his pouch and does a couple of tricks, Chapman is laughing and very amused with his friend's talent)*

Chapman
Hey Felicia, Cubby, come over here and see these neat magic tricks Billy can do.

Cubby
Bull E is upset that Felicia, Cubby and the other kids are watching Billy Bob. Cubby is sitting on stage eating, his back pack is a picnic basket and is engrossed in the card tricks, Bull E is between them) Hey Bull E, move out of my way so I can watch the tricks.

Bully E Moose
(Bull E becomes upset that Cubby would say that.) Hey there magic boy, why don't you make yourself disappear? *(The kids start moving away, like they have no choice but to leave, Chapman stays by Billy Bob.)*

Billy Bob
Who is that moose, Chapman? He ran into me in the hall and didn't even say he was sorry, and then he tripped me and knocked me over.

Chapman
Bull E Moose is the team pitcher and a very good athlete. He **thinks** he's 'cool'. Be careful around him. If you get on his bad side, there's no telling what he will do.

Billy Bob
Why is he like that?

Chapman
I don't know, but he is bigger and stronger than the rest of us, so we just stay out of his way and try to ignore his behavior. *(pause)* Let's get warmed up for tryouts. *(Chapman and Billy start tossing a ball. Miss Deer enters)*

Miss Dorrie Deer
Okay boys and girls, let's get started. *(To the audience)* it's time to talk about this year's team. Here's a little rule I want you all to remember; even though everyone gets to be part of the team, it's important we all work together. I want to make sure everyone understands the rules so we can all have a wonderful time.

Cubby
Time for the "bear facts"! *(The animal's chuckle)*

Miss Dorrie Deer
I want to remind you of our school's conduct rules (*or whatever your school calls the classroom rules*) *which we should always practice, whether we are in school or not. (To the audience)* Can anyone tell me what some of the values we should practice to make this a safe and fun game for everyone? *(The audience call out the values and the actors can fill in the blanks such as: play fair, be a good sport, be kind, courteous, helpful etc., be a good friend, listen for the values, and then repeat them.)* That's right; we all must be honest, respectful, responsible, caring and good sports. Remember the old saying, there is no "I" in Team!! *(Characters look at each other confused.)*

Cubby
T-E-A-M, Team, hey right! (he *counts on his fingers and figures out what the teacher was saying*)

Miss Deer
Let's play ball!! (*Chuckling and shaking her head at his joke*)

Scene 4

Place: on the playground, after the game. Everyone has left the stage except Felicia who hangs behind and watching from behind a tree.

Bull E Moose
Hey Possum, I gotta few words for you.

Billy Bob
Yes, Bull E?

Bull E Moose
(Bull E is tossing a small stone around Billy to intimidate him, but doesn't hit him with them) If I were you geek, I wouldn't come back to ball practice tomorrow and I wouldn't take a position on the team, *(pause, still tossing stones, walks around him and stares, Billy Bob is in awe.)* this is my game and my school. We don't need any weird marsupials like you here. You don't fit in here with your southern accent and your ugly pointy nose and that….. that, pocket of yours. I better not see you hanging around here either or I'll fix you, if you know what I mean. There's no room around here for you, so get lost and, oh, if you're thinking of telling anyone what I said I will knock you into the next county. These antlers aren't here just for beautiful looks; I know how to use them. *(Bull E. moves his antlers around like he is really proud of them. Billy begins to "play possum". This act is achieved by rolling over, shutting his eyes, opening his mouth, and going limp. He slumps down and stares at the ground without moving. Bull E stands over Billy Bob with intimidating power.)* Do you hear me Billy Bob? Billy Bob *(Bull E gently pokes him with his stick and Billy Bob doesn't move.)* Freak! *(Bull E walks off, shaking his head. Felicia runs off. There is a pause here before Chapman comes on.)*

Chapman
(Chapman enters looking for Billy Bob.)
Billy Bob! Has anyone seen Billy Bob? *(The audience points to Billy Bob and Chapman rushes over.)* Billy are you all right, what happened? *(Billy is trying to get up off the ground).*

Billy Bob
Oh, Chapman?

Chapman
Billy Bob what happen to you, are you all right, did you fall down?

Billy Bob
I'm okay, I ah. *(Not knowing what to say because he is embarrassed)* I just slipped on some pine needles, that's all.

Chapman
Are you sure? I can go get Miss Deer.

Billy Bob
No, I'm fine, go ahead and get your backpack and we'll walk home. *(Watching him closely, Chapman walks off, Billy looks around and moves up to sit on the stump, frightened that Bully E might come back. He begins to cry)* Boy, why do I feel so bad? Well this day didn't turn out like I thought it would. I was so excited about coming to *(your)* school. Chapman made it sound like so much fun. But ever since I got here, I have been made fun of for being different and having different habits than the other animals. I don't know what to do. I'm afraid and embarrassed to tell my mom and make her worry. I could tell Miss Deer *(hesitate, sniffles as to cry)* but if she talks to Bull E, he'll really hurt me and everyone will call me a tattletale. I guess the best thing to do is not play ball, I don't feel like it anyway. Maybe it will be better if I just stay away. I wish I was back at my old school where there are more people like me.

Chapman
(From off stage Chapman yells,) Come on Billy, let's go! *(Billy Bob exits sadly)*

Scene 5

In the kitchen at Billy Bob's house, Billy enters from his day at school and Mama is waiting with his favorite cookies.

Mama O

Billy how was your first day at school? Was it as exciting as you thought it would be? Did you meet some interesting animals? Tell me all about it?

Billy Bob

Yes Mom, you could say that.

Mama O

Billy Bob, what's wrong?

Billy Bob

(Crossing his fingers so Mama can't see) Nothing Mom, I'm really tired. I played stickball after school and I have lots of homework to do. I just want to go to my room and get the work done.

Mama O

Okay sweetie, but if something was bothering you, you would tell me, right?

Billy Bob

Right Mom

Scene 6

Outside Billy Bob's house or use the playground scenery.

Felicia
Hey Chapman, wait up. I need to talk to you. *(looking at his sad face)* What's wrong?

Chapman
I just walked Billy Bob home; I don't think he's feeling well.

Felicia
That's why I want to talk to you. What did you see?

Chapman
I found him lying down at Pine Tree Park; he looked scared, sick or something. He said he slipped on the pine needles.

Felicia
Well, I don't think he's sick but I do know what's wrong.

Chapman
Really, what is it?

Felicia
Well, after we finished playing stickball, I went back to the park to get my glove and I sort of listened to Bull E Moose and Billy Bob talking.

Chapman
What did they say?

Felicia
Bull E was telling Billy not to come back to the team. I thought Billy Bob was ignoring him. He just sat down and closed his eyes and then Bull E finally went away.

Chapman
Oh Felicia, he wasn't ignoring him. Billy Bob was playing possum.

Felicia
Possum, what's that?

Chapman
Well when opossums are afraid, they pretend to be dead. They will even look like they are dead. They fall over and sometime stick out their tongues, even drool.

Felicia
Wow, I never heard of that.

Chapman
Yes, so Billy Bob must have been very upset and scared of what Bull E was saying. Should we tell someone? I don't know what to do, Felicia!

Felicia
Me either, if we tell, we will be tattle tales and I don't want to get into trouble or have Bull E start calling me names.

Chapman
Ya, you're right, Bull E will probably stop anyway, don't you think?

Felicia
Well maybe, but I'm confused. I'll see you tomorrow at school. *(They hang their heads and walk off in different directions.)*

Scene 7

Cubby comes out with another sign that says, **The Next Morning.**
Place: Pine Tree Park. The next day at stickball practice, all players are standing to the side talking. Chapman and Felicia come on and approach each other. Bull E is right stage, up against a tree tossing a ball and catching it with his glove.

Chapman
Hi Felicia, how are you feeling today?

Felicia
Hi Chapman, well I didn't sleep much last night, how about you?

Chapman
Me neither, I'm very upset about Billy Bob and still don't know what to do.

Bull E Moose
(*From the other side of the stage*) It's a rattlesnake! Oh no, rattlesnakes are invading us too!! He's going to bite me!! (*everyone is upset and running around the stage not knowing what to do*)

Felicia
Don't move Bull E. Miss Deer, Miss Deer!!!!

Bull E Moose
Help! Help! Someone help me!

Everyone
(*All the characters are excited and upset and saying various things like "help, don't move", calling for the teacher. Have them run off stage*)

Miss Dorrie Deer
(*Running in hearing the excitement from the characters*) Now children, be calm, what's going on? (*Everyone talks at once telling her about Bull E*) Calm down children. Let's think of a way to handle this. Don't move Bull E. Kids stay back!

Billy Bob
(*Billy enters, sees the snake, grabs it and puts it in his pocket*) What's going on?

Chapman
It's Bull E, he was cornered by that rattlesnake you put in your pouch, and he's wasn't moving so he wouldn't get bit.

Chapman
Billy, how did you do that? You are awesome! You saved Bull E's life! (*Bull E is looking embarrassed and is now holding his head down and slumped over, breathing heavily.*)

Billy Bob
Do what?

Felicia
You certainly don't deserve it after the mean things you've been saying about Billy Bob.

Bull E Moose
(Out of breath, very relieved in a really low voice) Ya well ah…

Felicia
Bull E, you should get down on your knees and beg Billy for forgiveness.

Chapman
Yes, Bull E, you haven't been very nice to Billy since he moved here.

Bull E Moose
Well, um, Billy I…..

Billy Bob
Bull E…..

Miss Dorrie Deer
(Interrupting the conversation) What is going on here? Billy, has something happened I should know about? (*Billy says nothing*) Children? *(She looks from Billy to the audience and back to Billy. Audience starts telling the teacher that Bull E was bullying Billy Bob. Encourage the audience to tell the story by saying, "What's going on kids, can anyone tell me what's going on? " Listens and then addresses Billy Bob)* I know you don't know us very well but I only want to help you. If something has happen, no matter how big or little, I'm sure we can work it out together.

Felicia
(Tugging on Miss Deer) Billy Bob saved Bull E Moose from the rattlesnake and I think Bull E should be grateful and apologize to Billy Bob.

Miss Dorrie Deer
Apologize? Don't you mean say thank you?

Chapman
No, Miss Deer, Bull E has been threatening Billy Bob since he came to school here and then Billy ran in and saved his live.

Billy Bob
(*Trying to interrupt*) But um...

Miss Dorrie Deer
Well Bull E is there any truth to this*? (waits for an answer that doesn't come.)* Children you should have come to me about this.

Chapman
We didn't want to tattle, Miss Deer.

Miss Dorrie Deer
Tattling? (*Turning to Bull E)* Did you say inappropriate things to Billy Bob?

Bull E Moose
Well, um, I didn't really mean it, it's just when Billy Bob came to school and everyone was paying attention to him and were watching his magic tricks, it made me mad that he got all the attention. I didn't like that, usually everyone is watching me play ball and telling me how good I am. So I thought if I told Billy not to try out for the team, he would get scared and go away. I didn't say it to hurt anyone.

Cubby
Bull E you're always bullying and teasing others. By the way, my name is Cubby, not Chubby! *(pause and looks at Miss Deer)* Miss Deer, he calls me names all the time.

Felicia
That's right Miss Deer, he did say mean things to Billy Bob, I heard it myself.

Chapman
Felicia and I talked about it yesterday. We really couldn't decide what to do. It was very confusing and made us feel really bad.

Miss Dorrie Deer
Well, okay, it's good that you are telling me this now. Bull E, I think it is best that you and I discuss this in private with your parents and the principal.

Bull E Moose
(*Hesitating*) I... um, yes Miss Deer.

Billy Bob
.. Chapman, Miss Deer, everyone..... listen to me. This is NOT a rattlesnake and I DIDN'T save his life! First of all this is an Eastern Milk Snake and even if it were a rattlesnake, opossums are immune to rattlesnake venom.

Bull E Moose
What!??

Billy Bob
…… that's right. If I get a rattlesnake bite, it won't hurt me. Opossums don't get sick from snakebites. We hunt rattlesnakes as part of our diet. Anyways I'm no hero; I was just hunting for something to eat.

Chapman
Oh yeah, that's right, don't you remember what Billy Bob said the first day of school, when he told the class about the habits of opossums? *(others shake their head agreeing)*

Miss Dorrie Deer
Nonetheless, this is something we need to discuss. Helping someone who hasn't been very kind is an act of good citizenship, whether the snake was poisonous or not. Billy Bob, would you like to tell me in your own words what happened?

Felicia
Go ahead Billy; you're safe with all of us here. Tell Miss Deer what happened at stickball the other day.

Billy Bob
Well, *(hesitates, looks around, at first he is afraid to talk, but starts out slowly, moves to center stage)* Bull E you did hurt my feelings *(pause)* and I felt like I didn't want to live here anymore. I didn't feel safe at school and wanted to stay home. I was very excited about moving here and meeting new friends. Although I met great new folks like Chapman, Cubby and Felicia, I still was scared to come to school. I thought I did something wrong. I didn't dare to tell anyone. I didn't want to be a tattletale either. I just didn't know what to do, so that's why I haven't been at stickball all week. I just figured ya'll wouldn't miss me and I could avoid being around Bull E.

Miss Dorrie Deer
Billy, remember that you can always go to a teacher, parents or an adult you trust for help. We are only looking out for your best interest! *(turns to all the animals)* And about the tattling, it's important to remember that if a person is getting hurt by a situation, then it is not tattling. *(Characters look at each other, surprised by this)*

Billy Bob
I didn't know that. I felt strange inside, it was a funny feeling I just couldn't figure it out. I thought I did something wrong.

Miss Deer
(Miss Deer gathers the animals together to talk with them, you can use this speech or have Miss Deer ask the students of ways to solve the problem, or use both, sometimes with younger children, some of the dialog will be too long to keep their attention,) Children, I know you are confused. Remember our talk at the stickball game? Being respectful and fair is the only way we can all get along.

Miss Deer

Accepting others for who they are helps us understand everyone's differences. We then find out that we're all not so different after all. You see, when we tease or bully someone, it creates bad feelings, not only to that person, but to others around them, the bystanders. It's okay to ask for help and a big step towards solving the problem. Ignoring or trying to handle it on your own can be harmful and sometime dangerous. *(Characters again look at Miss Deer with questioning expressions.)*

Felicia

Billy, I want to apologize to you.

Billy Bob

Why, Felicia? You didn't do anything.

Felicia

That's right, I didn't do anything! You see, Billy, I should have told someone what Bull E was doing sooner. I just ignored him hoping he would stop bullying. I didn't want to say anything because I was afraid he would tease me too. From now on, I will try to be a good citizen and ask an adult when someone needs help. No more bystanding for me, from now on you can count on me as, a …. STANDbyer, ya, that's it, a **STANDbyer!!**

Cubby

Me too, Billy Bob, I'll try hard to be a good friend to everyone.

Chapman

That goes for me too Billy Bob. *(speaks to the rest of the kids in the audience)* Well I don't know about you guys, but I'm really glad that Billy Bob migrated here. I've learned so much. It's important to respect and honor others for who they are. Now I understand what the school conduct means. We can learn a lot more by listening and respecting others.

Miss Deer

I know this is a great deal to think about. How about we set aside a time each week to talk about expected classroom behaviors and the way we want our school climate to be.

Cubby

Well, I know I want my "climate" to be warm and fuzzy!

Everyone

Yeah, okay, sounds good to me!

Miss Deer

Okay then, but in the meantime, if you have a question or problem……. *(Cubby cuts her off)*

Cubby

We'll come to you, Miss Deer! Now let's play some ball! *(the animals all yell, 'Yeah', and pick up their gloves and exit the stage.*

The End!

Production Notes

Casting Notes

Classroom Preparation

Most or all-bullying takes place when an adult is not within hearing or observing distance or children are unsupervised. This program empowers children and youth to stand up for themselves in a bullying or harassment situation. Supporting and empowering children to practice positive social behaviors like honesty, fairness, integrity, empathy, compassion, respect and responsibility for their own actions will result in a healthy school environment. Here are a few ideas when preparing for the play.

1. Inform students and parents of the programs expectations and the purpose for the production. Suggest the discussion continue at home by giving the parents talking tips. State your expectations and outcomes to both students and parents.

2. Review your State, school or program policy on harassment and bully prevention.

3. Review the definition of bullying, many adults are surprised at some of the incidents that are classified as discrimination, bullying or harassment. Be sure to understand the definition of bullying and how you can empower the students. Suggested reading for this is *The Comfort Zone, Providing a safe and bully free environment for school age childcare by* Robin D'Antona, Ed.D., Meline Kevorkian Ed.D., and Deb Landry. Bryson Taylor Publishing offers many bullying prevention books and plays, visit the website for more information.

4. Design your own list of questions to ask before and after the play that are unique to your program. A list of references and questions are available in this workbook.

5. Prepare a pre and post questionnaire to assist in monitoring classroom or school improvement. This is a great tool for monitoring, reporting and grant proposals.

6. Use a behavior rubric for monitoring and follow up on a weekly and monthly basis. Follow up is vital and necessary.

7. Reporting may increases after the presentation. Reported incidents will decrease with awareness and when the classroom expectations are practiced and respected. Guidelines for a positive outcome in a behavior plan should include clear, explicit, positive behavior expectations and boundaries.

Classroom Expectations

Here are some expectations:

- Students will recognize key differences between appropriate and inappropriate social behaviors
- Experience or develop a mentoring relationship with trusted adult, peers or older student
- Clarify difference between bystander reporting vs. tattling
- Identify bullying
- Accountability, expressing feelings and work out problems through character role play
- Healthy tips on what students can do if they or someone they know is being bullied
- How teachers and adults fit into this equation by listening and setting positive examples of behavior
- Students learn the different habits of northeastern animals. Pointing out the differences in the animals can also be compared to how we are all different individuals and how we/they respectfully cohabitate
- Importance of communication with teachers and parents
- Improved listening skills
- Value of ongoing communication between teachers and students on expected classroom, school and community behavior
- How to build trusting relationships

Be a STAND-byer!

Classroom Discussion and Questions

Sticks Stones and Stumped portrays the problem of one student's power over another. The program offers solutions in a safe, effective tone and explores the difference between tattling and reporting a potential bullying incident. Empowering students to understand what bullying and harassment is and the power in reporting will result in students taking responsibility for their actions. The following questions are examples for classroom discussion.

- Changing the language can sometimes help; try using the word "reporting" instead of telling.

- The animals can be used as part of a project. Discuss the animals, their habits and differences. Compare how they live together in their community.

- Follow up with post presentation worksheets available in this manual or create your own. Fun and repetitive activities will remind students of the desired outcome and appropriate behaviors.

- What is bullying? What are some of the ways children are bullied? Billy Bob was very excited about the first day of school but things didn't turn out the way he thought they would. What happened? What are some feelings he may have had while waiting for Chapman, while telling the class about his family, meeting new friends and when Bully E Moose made comments.

- Why do you think Bull E said mean things to Billy Bob? Is there a reason? Does it matter, and does he have the right to say inappropriate comments to Billy Bob? Why?

- Why didn't Chapman and Felicia ask for help? Maybe because they didn't understand the difference between tattling and reporting?

- Chapman said "Bull E thinks he's cool." Is it cool to be a bully, why, why not?

- Where are some of the places kids get bullied? Discuss bus safety and hot spots in the school. Why do you think people that bully don't bully kids in front of teachers or adults? Do you think your teachers or parents know when someone is bullied if you don't tell them?

- What are some examples of the actions you can take if you are bullied? Or what are some of the actions you should/shouldn't take? Example: Tell them to stop, ignore them, walk away and tell an adult you can trust.

- Ask: have you ever been a bully, seen someone get bullied or have been bullied yourself? If so raise your hand. Let them see how many hands are up. You will find that some students do not raise their hand. Some students see bullying as a bigger kid picking on a smaller kid. Be sure to explain the many types of bullying and harassment like: name-calling, exclusion, girl fighting, cyberbullying and rumors. You may want to ask this question first and then repeat it after the presentation is completed. You will see that the number increases significantly if they didn't understand what bullying was before the presentation.

- How does it make you feel when you see others get teased or bullied? If you could do something, what would it be?

- What are some safe ways you could help a friend who is bullied? Explain how to ask for help and why it is important. Adults ask for help everyday, give some examples on how adults ask for help for others.

- Role-play: Identify a problem and see how successful the students are at solving it. This can be done by pretending to be Billy Bob, Chapman and Bull E Moose. Encourage students to brainstorm possible solutions. When appropriate, help the students think of other possible solutions and remind them of classroom rules and school's climate expectations. Listen to and respect all of their ideas.

- Who gets hurt when someone is bullied? How? And why?

- Intervene in the moment. When children are inappropriate, Chuck Saufler, bullying prevention trainer and guidance counselor says an in the moment intervention is helpful such as: "we don't do that here" will make a significant difference and remind students of the expected behavior. They will soon understand that it is inappropriate and learn or be reminded of acceptable school behaviors.

Costumes

When using the book as part of the play try to match the animal's clothes and attire with the characters. You can also use you local team uniforms.

All
Baseball Hats with "C" on the hats for Crossroads Critters or use your school name or mascot. Billy Bob would have a different colored hat with an "O" for Oklahoma Oakies.

Backpacks, primary colored long sleeved T-shirts, jeans and sneakers, and knit gloves for paws. Any body part exposed should be made out of fur or felt the color of the animal. Headpieces can be made out of foam or fur and attached to a headband.

Billy Bob
- Add a large pouch to the costume for his odds and ends
- Long pink tail and nose
- Do not wear pants over the costume so he can use his pouch.
- Billy Bob uses his pouch instead of a backpack.

Bull E Moose
- Antlers, big
- Dress in blue jeans and a flannel shirt with hiking boots
- Work gloves for hands

Miss Deer
- Skirt or dress, no antlers
- Brown stockings and long sleeve turtleneck
- Matching black shoes and gloves for the hooves
- A whistle on a lanyard with buttons promoting school spirit
- Ball cap for stickball scenes

Props

- Signs with directions to school and park
- Stickball bats and baseball gloves
- Rocks and stones as balls, regular rubber or plastic balls spray painted gray or covered with gray duct tape
- 2 stumps for school chairs and a board to connect the stumps in the park, which doubles as a stickball bench
- Backpacks and a picnic basket as Cubby's backpack with a blanket
- Bell and pad of paper & pencil
- Clipboard for teacher/coach and a whistle
- School books
- Large rubber snake
- Magic cards and odds and ends for Billy Bob's pouch

Production Tips

Teachers Guide to Sticks Stones & Stumped Interactive Play

Suggested groups for casting: utilize middle or high school students, teachers, drama clubs, civil rights clubs, peer mediation groups, student council, reader's theater for a classroom, or upper classmates.

Use your imagination: Feel free to add characters, lines and specific problems your school may be experiencing. Example: name-calling. **Encourage Adlibbing**

What and When to say it: The name of the character who speaks is in the center of the page with the character's line immediately underneath. An example is as follows:

Felicia
Really? Wow, I never heard of that.

Chapman
Yes, so Billy Bob must have been very upset and scared of what Bull E. was doing or what he was saying. Should we tell someone? I don't know what to do!

Suggestions: Cut and copy the student script and have the student highlight all their characters lines and the last few words of the line before they are to speak.

Who's Who

Character descriptions:

Bull E. Moose: *The bully. Should be taller than others, doesn't smile*

Billy Bob Opossum: *The new kid in school, southern accent, the target*

Miss Dorrie Deer: *Teacher and stickball coach*

Chapman the Chipmunk: *Billy's friend, a bystander*

Felicia Fox: *A friend and bystander*

Cubby Bear: *A silly bear and bystander have Cubby learn some "Knock, Knock" jokes and come out before the show starts to warm up the audience, as the show starts, he can slowly join the actors.*

Mama O: *Billy Bob's Mom, can be doubled as Dorrie Dear*
Add other nonspeaking roles such as rabbits, raccoons, and groundhogs.

Scenery painted by

Amy Cote

Scenery can be painted on canvas, large cardboard boxes, cardboard or on three 4x8 pieces of plywood. Hinge together with a triangle and turn with each scene.

Teacher to Parent Communication

Students perform better in school when teachers openly communicate with parents, when parents become actively involved in their children's education and when a healthy school climate is maintained. Close communications with parents and strong leadership skills from the teacher can significantly improve the school climate, educational experience, and follow the students throughout their lives.

There are a number of ways that teachers can communicate with parents rather than relying on the scheduled parent-teacher conferences or waiting until a bullying or harassment situation occurs. Creating clear boundaries, ground rules and strong respectable relationships will foster positive and committed strategies when problems arise. Teachers and parents must create positive behaviors and clear expectations students can obtain and comprehend. The teacher- parent relationship must set a good example by following the same expectations used for the students and with the same values outlined in the school's rules. The following guidelines will assist and facilitate positive, clear expectations for all involved while contributing to a safe school climate. These tips for communication and organization are the first steps in the prevention of behavioral issues, bullying, harassment, sexual harassment, bias-based harassment, discrimination, age, gender and cultural sensitivities.

Key points to effective teacher to parent communication

- **Open the lines of communication:** Teachers should welcome meeting their students' parents early in the school year. Making an effort to do this will help the teacher better understand the student and parent. Understanding the family's dynamics positively supports the education of the student. Inform parents how you teach and manage your classroom. Clearly and kindly set your classroom boundaries. Be tactful, flexible, clear and honest. Being respectful, honest and direct will help set the atmosphere and expectations of your parents.

- **Outline communication expectations:** Begin the year with both an open house and welcome letter. Sponsor a school wide open house where everyone can meet and hear from all the departments in the school. (Principal, teachers, unified arts teachers, school organizations, bus and lunch programs). Communicate both verbally and also in a hand out that parents can refer to at a later date. Include contact information such as email address, school telephone number, address, website, key personnel, the best time for contacting and who they should contact for specific issues. Discuss and outline appropriate times and desired ways of contact. Inform parents when guest speakers like bully prevention programs are going on, encourage parents to talk to the student about the program at home. Make classroom expected behavior ongoing conversation with students and parents.

- **Consistent and organized communication:** Supply consistent, scheduled and organized communication such as written, newsletters, teacher's website or email on a weekly basis. Clearly outline to parents and students the school and classroom expectations. Inform parents what organizations and policies are available and make them accessible. Along with frequent classroom newsletters include: Principal's newsletter, PTO/PTA newsletters, school websites, email addresses, year at a glance, changes in the schedule, how the grading system works and school homework hotlines/websites. Parents and students need to understand how and where to get their questions answered. Lines of communication must always be practiced so when parents and students have a concern, they do not become frustrated searching for an answer or trying to understand how to communicate with the teacher. Defuse defensive behavior by clearly stating your intentions, rules and process.

- **Initial and ongoing face-to-face meetings and encounters:** Parent-teacher conferences are often scheduled at the time of the first report card in the school year. For parents and teachers, this is a chance to talk one-on-one about the student. The parent-teacher conference is a good opportunity to review the partnership between student, parent and teacher but should not be the first and only face-to-face encounter, especially if there are problems or issues that will take more than the fifteen minutes allotted. Beyond the open house, teachers and staff should be visible, available, and welcoming to parents and students during school visits, drop off and pick up times. For the students; teachers, staff and administration should make themselves visible in hallways, during the changing of classes, recesses, lunch and dismissal. Staff should be identifiable immediately with nametags or employee identification badges.

- **Documentation:** Beyond grades, keep accurate records of handouts, parent letters and on individual student communication, such as difficult, unusual or disruptive behavior, grades, missing assignments, outstanding behaviors, telephone and written communications with parents. Address your concerns early. Listen to what your parent and students have to say about respective bullying and harassment incidents. Partner with your principal, assistant principal, school counselor, or a respected past teacher for advice or their experience and understanding if problems arise. Let parents know of potential concerns and always balance this with the positive attributes you are observing. Parents should get more positive information than negative about their children.

- **School and Student Organizations:** Participate and encourage parents to join parent-teacher organizations such as PTO, PTA and the Booster Clubs. Teachers can enhance parent communication by participating in these organizations. As all parents do not get actively involved, not all teachers need to attend. Assigning consistent school representation is vital. In larger schools a teacher representative from each class or department can be responsible for communication between the organizations members and rotate on a regular basis. Attend school-sponsored events or host a classroom project designed to get parents involved. Encourage students to be involved in school activities such as civil rights groups, peer mediation or leadership groups. Be consistent in attendance and visible.

- **Volunteers and Teamwork:** Depending upon parent's availability, interests, and the needs of the school, the opportunities are endless. Some suggestions include: chaperones, fundraising, hall and lunchroom monitoring, tutoring, copying, library aides, classroom speaker on a specific topic of interest, organizing papers to go home, typing, and concession worker at school events. Teachers should take stock of their parents' skills and interests to volunteer and ask the parent how they can volunteer. Spend time organizing your classroom and find tasks or projects that parents can do weekly. Build a team with you at the helm. The tasks are endless, teachers can focus on the students and parents feel engaged. Increase adult supervision assists in decreasing bullying and harassment.

- **Understanding diversity:** Understand and address cultural issues in your community, school and classroom. Acknowledged and respected behavior should be consistently demonstrated to parents and students. Respectfully leave personal opinions out of the school climate. This behavior will positively affect parents and students.

- **Media Impact:** Encourage and educate parents on media impact. Media need not be violent or disruptive to affect the learning process for students and also their communication skills. Work with parents to encourage decreasing the time spent on video games and television with more time allocated to reading and participation in projects, whether school or community.

Note: The Parent Teacher Communication article authored by Deb Landry, is part of the Maine State Best Practices in Bullying and Harassment Prevention Manual. The manual, including a sample law and reference list is available as a download on our website at www.brysontaylorpublishing.com.

Students are
Respectable, Responsible, Honest
Compassionate, Caring, Courageous
Fair, Kind, Good Citizens and

STANDbyers

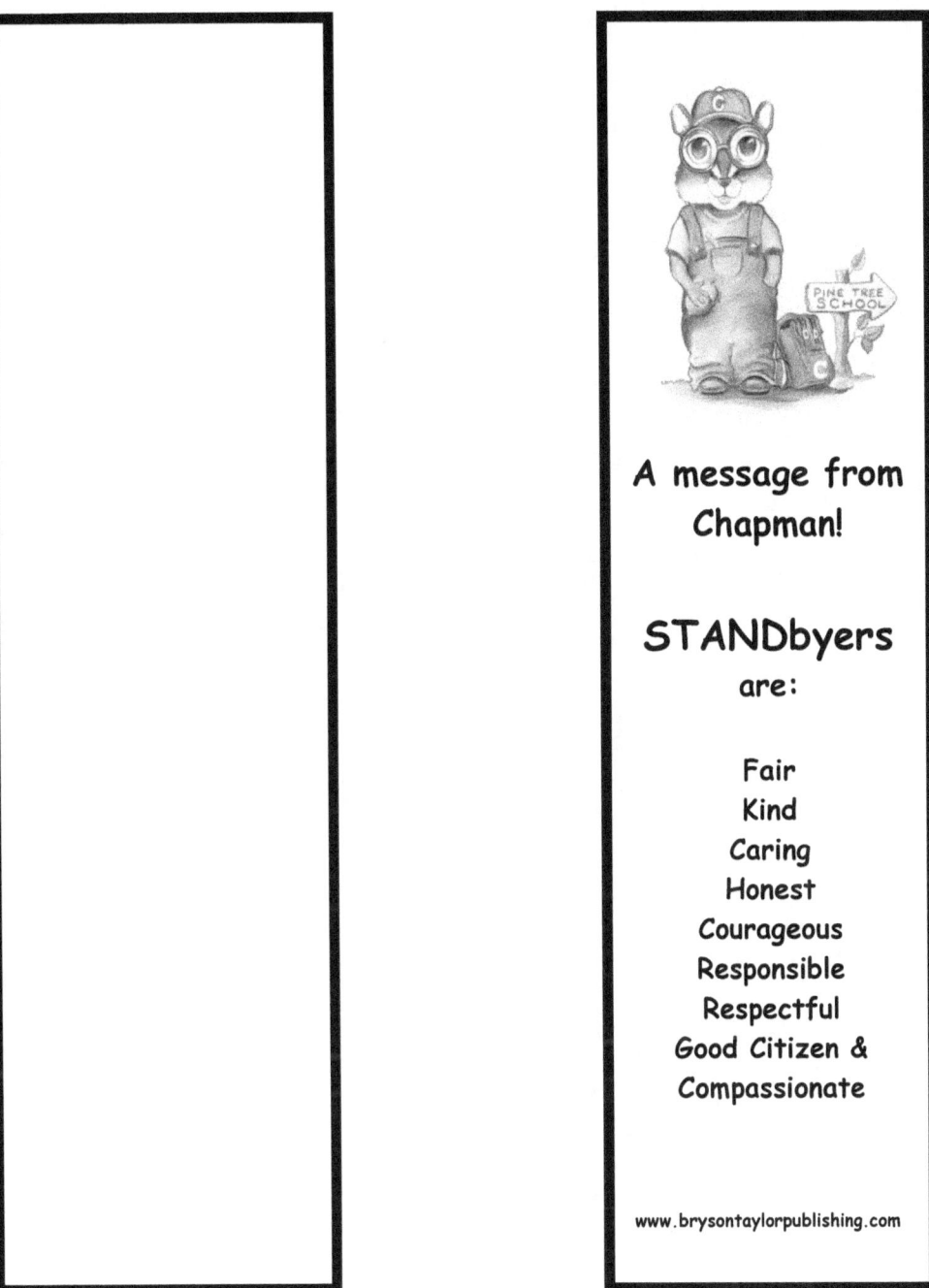

A message from Chapman!

STANDbyers
are:

Fair
Kind
Caring
Honest
Courageous
Responsible
Respectful
Good Citizen &
Compassionate

www.brysontaylorpublishing.com

Design your own bookmark and school poster. Add your school's name, and laminate the poster on page 29. Make several copies to hang around the school as a reminder. When hanging posters throughout the school, be sure to move them on a regular basis so they don't become part of the general scenery. For the bookmarks, cut, color, personalize, glue and laminate. Add your own school or classroom mottos.

Color posters and bookmarks are available on our website or by email
info@brysontaylorpublishing.com

STANDbyer Fallen Phrases

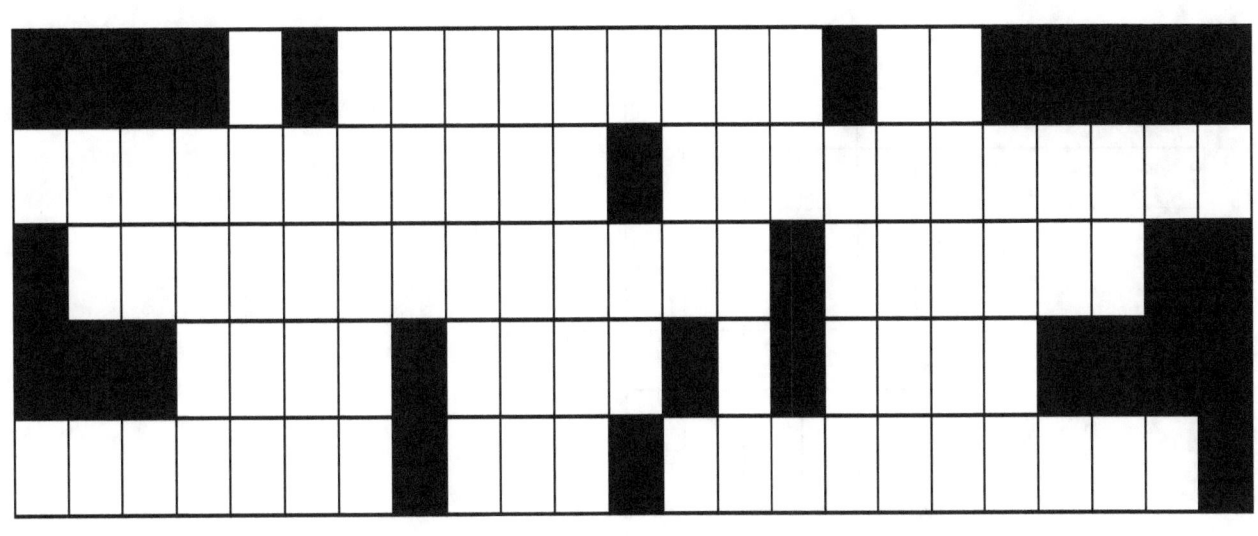

Bully Facts
Sticks, Stones and Stumper!

Across
1. The target in Sticks Stones and Stumped.
3. The teacher at Pine Tree School.
5. Bill Bob's new friend.

Down
1. The story's bully.
2. The bystander that apologized to Billy Bob.
4. Stickball is a g____.

Here is a get to know everyone exercise for the classroom.

Be creative when posting each students name. On a large poster design a large apple tree with colored paper. Find out three things about each student in your classroom by teaming two students at a time and having them talk about themselves for a minute or two. Then have one student introduce their partner to the class and tell their story. This exercise will help them get to know each other and also find some commonality. They can then work together to write their names with their interest on the apple. Don't forget the teacher and other helpers in the classroom. Play this game periodically until each student has talked with everyone in the class including you! Change posters with the seasons.

On the apple have the student write the name of their partner and three important facts about them and glue it to their personal tree. Creating a safe environment will improve the dynamics of the classroom. Copy, enlarge, or draw your own tree, glue apples accordingly.

Classic Stumper Word Find

Find and Circle the words listed below

```
A I H M B C V N W R N M M F B
X I F O U J U Z E N N A O S Y
Y Y C B N R C E X S A M E S S
J L B I E E D X B E M M E D T
S Y L M L E S I S S P A E Z A
H T O U I E L T J O A O R Y N
S H I R B L F E Y O H Z T T D
U T R C Y Z M L K M C H E V E
V O K B K R E S P E C T Q B R
D U O C K B P T N L E N I A M
L B B E E Q A W T L A Z O V N
N D N G B S Q L S U Q J X I P
M U S S O P O I L B V Q U H E
C R O S S R O A D S Y C F J X
X Z P R H U N F D I A P N O H
```

BILLY BOB	BULL E MOOSE	BULLY	BYSTANDER
CHAPMAN	CROSSROADS	CUBBY	DORRIE DEER
FELICIA	HOMERUN	HONESTY	MAINE
MAMMA O	OPOSSUM	RESPECT	STICKBALL
TREE			

Special Message!

Make a Sentence

| A | S | H | AVE | SUP | IAL | MAR | CH. | POU |

| | | | | | | | |

| ULL | A | B | Y | N | Y. | A | B | UDD | OT | BE |

| | | | | | | | |

Possum Facts

Did you know?

Only female opossums have a pouch.
Opossums are the only marsupials in North America.
Opossums don't hang from trees by their tales, only very small newborn opossums do this!
The North American Opossum is also known as the Virginia Opossum.
Opossums "clean up" the woods by eating things like the dead animals, mice, rats, and berries.
Opossums really do "play dead" if they are threatened!
They have two rows of teeth totaling fifty in all.

Take Home Booklet Instructions:

The next two pages are back to back take home booklets. Copy the pages back to back, cut horizontally, fold together and staple in the fold.

Billy Bob's Favorite Butternut Cookies

2 cups butter
2 cups brown sugar
2 eggs
2 tsp. vanilla
1 tsp. baking soda
1/2 tsp. baking powder
1/2 tsp. salt
3 cups flour
1 cup chopped pecans**

Frosting
1/2 cup browned butter -- reserved*
2 tsp. vanilla
3 cups powdered sugar
1/4 cup hot water
* Reserve 1/2 cup browned butter for frosting
** 2/3 cup if measuring chopped pecans

Brown butter in deep saucepan. The butter will melt, then bubble, then foam, then turn nut-brown quickly thereafter. Remove from heat. Reserve 1/2 cup browned butter for frosting.
Beat browned butter and brown sugar together until the browned butter isn't hot any more. Add eggs, vanilla, baking soda, baking powder, and salt; beat thoroughly. Add 3 cups flour and chopped pecans, and mix well. Drop by tablespoons onto ungreased cookie sheet. Bake at 350 degrees 10 minutes.
Combine frosting ingredients, beat well, and spread over cooled cookies.

A children's book and educational interactive program on bullying prevention
**Contact us at
838-2146
www.brysontaylorpubishing.com**

Draw the characters

Draw a picture of a Safe School

How many nuts in Mamma O's butternut cookies?

Draw your favorite Character

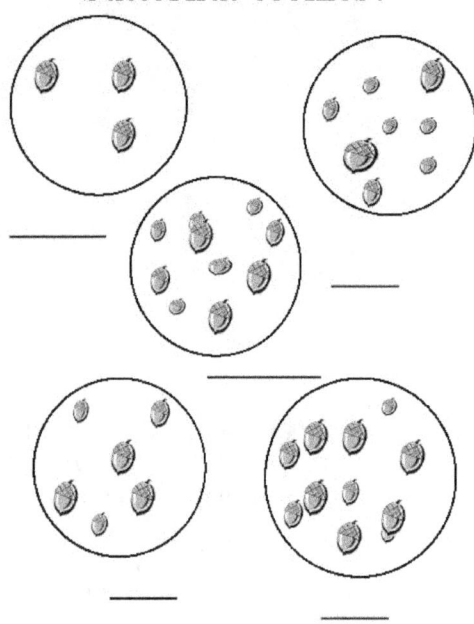

Help Miss Deer unscramble the sentences……..

Enoyever si rteneffid.

_____

Eb a tnasbdiye

_____

Letl na duatl uyo rutts

_____

Sticks Stones and Stumper!

```
F F K B R Y L L U B
F E L I C I A F U Y
C N Y L H T A L Z S
P D T L A C L F Z T
A D S Y P E S F A A
Q C E B M P S R P N
P T N O A S G I E D
A V O B N E Q E Z E
K S H P T R B N C R
E J D D K I N D T R
```

Billy Bob
Bull E
Moose
Bully
Target
Chapman
Felicia
Friend
Fair
Honesty
Kind
Respect
Bystander

Find and circle the words to the right.

Sticks Stones and Stumped!

Pledge Certificate

I pledge to do my best to be a Standbyer by being fair, honest, compassionate, responsible and respectful to my classmates and my school.

_____

You are here by declared a

STANDbyer!

Presented on this day _____

By _____

An educational interactive children's play on bullying and harassment prevention

DEB LANDRY

Sticks, Stones and Stumped!
THE PLAY

STUDENT SCRIPT

NAME

CHARACTER

Sticks, Stones and Stumped!

Interactive Children's Bullying and Harassment Prevention Play

By Deb Landry

Scene 1

Description: Billy Bob Opossum has migrated to Maine from the south. He is excited about his first day at school and meeting his new teacher and classmates.

Place: In the kitchen of Billy Bob's new tree house.

Mama O
(*Mama O speaks with a southern accent. She wears an apron, which can have a couple of stuffed opossums sticking out of the pockets. She is cleaning up around the kitchen, looks around and doesn't see Billy Bob*) Billy Bob, it's time to get ready for school. Don't forget to brush your teeth and make your bed.

Billy Bob
(*Jumps up from behind the stage, fully dress and taps Mama on the shoulder, he speaks in a southern accent, smiles to show his clean teeth*) Here I am Mama O. I'm all ready for school and have all my chores done! I'm so excited I just couldn't sleep any longer.

Mama O
Oh, Billy Bob you look so handsome! Do you have your lunch and your... (*Billy interrupts*).

Billy Bob
Mama I have everything. (*Patting his pouch, Billy has on a baseball hat; he does not carry a backpack*) I'm going to walk with Chapman. He said he would introduce me to his friends and we would have so much fun, especially at recess time and playing stickball.

(*There is a knock on the door.*)Billy goes to answer the door, hurrying with excitement.)

Billy Bob
Hey, Chapman

Chapman
Hey Billy Bob, Mrs. O, are you ready to go?

Billy Bob
Ya! I can't wait, let's get going.
(*They run off stage. Mama smiles at the boys and waves goodbye.*)

Scene 2

Place: Inside the classroom of Miss Dorrie Deer. Scenery can be inside of a tree with stumps as desks. See samples of scenery on page 17. Cubby Bear and Felicia Fox enter and sit on their stumps making small talk. Billy Bob and Chapman then enter and Billy is introduced to Felicia Fox, Cubby Bear, and the rest of the class, which is the audience. (Bull E Moose, can be seated in the audience, eavesdrops on the conversation by making an earlier entrance before the show or he can make a grand entrance later). Billy and Chapman are standing, Felicia and Cubby stand up to be introduced, draws attention to them. If Bull E is in the audience, he should ask the children to be quiet so he can hear what is going on.

Chapman
Billy Bob, these are my friends Felicia and Cubby. They play on my stickball team the Critters.

Felicia
Hi Billy Bob, welcome to *"Your School". (Insert your school name.)*

Cubby
Hey Billy Bob, Knock, Knock,

Billy Bob
Who's there?

Cubby
Spell

Billy Bob
Spell Who?

Cubby
W-H-O! *(They all laugh)*

Billy Bob
It's very nice to meet ya'll. *(Billy is chuckling; Felicia and Cubby sit back down in front of Bull E. Billy and Chapman sit in the front of the class on their stumps.)*

Felicia
Hey, Billy and Chapman, want to play with us at recess time? *(They nod yes with excitement.)*

Miss Dorrie Deer
Children, children, (*interrupting the conversation* and *ringing a bell, Miss Dorrie Deer comes in behind the audience or walking in from outside the classroom*) please stop talking and get to your seat, we need to get started. *(Children respond to the bell and begin to find a place to sit; the children in the audience are also included as they are part of the classroom. Dorrie walks through the audience checking to see that all children are quiet, listening and ready to learn, she talks to the children with a kind voice. She begins the dialog when she is in front of the class.)* Thank you very much children, it is so nice to see all of you after the long winter hibernation break. Welcome back! Before we get started with our class, I would like to introduce our new student, Billy Bob Opossum. *(Motions for Billy Bob to stand and children clap and yell from the audience. Felicia, Cubby and Chapman should start the applause, giving the other children permission to clap also, Bull E moves closer and joins the set)* Billy Bob, tell us a little about yourself and where you lived before you came to Maine.

Billy Bob
(*Smiling shyly*) Well Miss Dear, our family migrated here from Oklahoma. (*He continues to talk but can't be heard by anyone because Bull E is talking. Dorrie and Chapman, Felicia and Cubby listen, smiling with interest and shaking their heads to what Billy is saying, they cannot hear what Bull E. is saying to the audience*)

Bull E Moose
Well maybe he should go back "homa". What a weirdo, what kind of animal is he anyway? He's really ugly, and listen to the way he talks! *(Felicia gasps and looks disgusted at Bull E., scene goes back to Billy.)*

Billy Bob
….and I like to play stickball, do magic and collect odds and ends to store here in my pouch. Back home I was the catcher (*pulling out his stone ball out of his pouch*) on the Oakies and made 10 home runs last year! *(Billy Bob continues to talk but can't be heard)*

Bull E Moose
Big deal what a bragger, he's probably making up stories. Ten homeruns! Sure. And what's up with that pouch, I've never seen anything like that, I can imagine what else he keeps in there. What a flea infested nuisance.

Felicia
Stop it Bull E. It's not nice to say things like that. You don't want to hurt his feelings, do you? You know Billy Bob is harmless and seems like a very friendly guy.

Bull E Moose
Well, he's making up all these stories, I know he is.

Felicia
How do you know that? Anyway, we can always use another catcher and base runner for our team.

Cubby
Hey, I'm all for someone running the bases for me!

Bull E Moose
Not if I have anything to say about it. We're fine just the way we are. He can sit on the stump and keep score with *Chubby*. Better yet, he doesn't need to come at all.

Miss Dorrie Deer
Thank you, Billy Bob; we are very happy to have you here, right boys and girls?

Everyone except Bull E Moose
Yeah! *(Everyone claps)*

Miss Dorrie Deer
I hope you will like your new school and friends. Let me know if you need help. *(Billy sits down)* Okay children, today at recess we will have the tryouts for the spring stickball team. Anyone that is interested in playing on the Critter Team, meet me at the Pine Tree clearing field after school. Billy, I hope you will join the team! *(Billy and Chapman look at each other, shake their heads yes and smile excitedly)*

Bull E Moose
(Bragging) Well I guess we know who's going to be the star pitcher again this year! *(Looking around the room at everyone)* Don't bother trying out boys and girls, I've got this all wrapped up. *(Classmates look at each other puzzled).*

Miss Dorrie Deer
Okay children let's take out our nature book and get ready for our tree identification quiz! *(All the students respond with an: oh no.)*

Scene 3

In between scenes, Cubby Bear brings out a sign that says, **Later that afternoon.** *He can have it upside down or side ways, something to make the kids laugh. Place: Pine Tree Park. Bull E is tossing the ball by himself center stage, taking up a lot of space, showing off. The other characters are around the stage in various places.*

Billy Bob
Hey Chapman, want to see a magic trick? *(Billy pulls out some cards from his pouch and does a couple of tricks, Chapman is laughing and very amused with his friend's talent)*

Chapman
Hey Felicia, Cubby, come over here and see these neat magic tricks Billy can do.

Cubby
Bull E is upset that Felicia, Cubby and the other kids are watching Billy Bob. Cubby is sitting on stage eating, his back pack is a picnic basket and is engrossed in the card tricks, Bull E is between them) Hey Bull E, move out of my way so I can watch the tricks.

Bully E Moose
(Bull E becomes upset that Cubby would say that.) Hey there magic boy, why don't you make yourself disappear? *(The kids start moving away, like they have no choice but to leave, Chapman stays by Billy Bob.)*

Billy Bob
Who is that moose, Chapman? He ran into me in the hall and didn't even say he was sorry, and then he tripped me and knocked me over.

Chapman
Bull E Moose is the team pitcher and a very good athlete. He **thinks** he's 'cool'. Be careful around him. If you get on his bad side, there's no telling what he will do.

Billy Bob
Why is he like that?

Chapman
I don't know, but he is bigger and stronger than the rest of us, so we just stay out of his way and try to ignore his behavior. *(pause)* Let's get warmed up for tryouts. *(Chapman and Billy start tossing a ball. Miss Deer enters)*

Miss Dorrie Deer
Okay boys and girls, let's get started. *(To the audience)* it's time to talk about this year's team. Here's a little rule I want you all to remember; even though everyone gets to be part of the team, it's important we all work together. I want to make sure everyone understands the rules so we can all have a wonderful time.

Cubby
Time for the "bear facts"! *(The animal's chuckle)*

Miss Dorrie Deer
I want to remind you of our school's conduct rules (*or whatever your school calls the classroom rules*) which we should always practice, whether we are in school or not. *(To the audience)* Can anyone tell me what some of the values we should practice to make this a safe and fun game for everyone? *(The audience call out the values and the actors can fill in the blanks such as: play fair, be a good sport, be kind, courteous, helpful etc., be a good friend, listen for the values, and then repeat them.)* That's right; we all must be honest, respectful, responsible, caring and good sports. Remember the old saying, there is no "I" in Team!! *(Characters look at each other confused.)*

Cubby
T-E-A-M, Team, hey right! (he *counts on his fingers and figures out what the teacher was saying*)

Miss Deer
Let's play ball!! (*Chuckling and shaking her head at his joke*)

Scene 4

Place: on the playground, after the game. Everyone has left the stage except Felicia who hangs behind and watching from behind a tree.

Bull E Moose
Hey Possum, I gotta few words for you.

Billy Bob
Yes, Bull E?

Bull E Moose
(Bull E is tossing a small stone around Billy to intimidate him, but doesn't hit him with them) If I were you geek, I wouldn't come back to ball practice tomorrow and I wouldn't take a position on the team, *(pause, still tossing stones, walks around him and stares, Billy Bob is in awe.)* this is my game and my school. We don't need any weird marsupials like you here. You don't fit in here with your southern accent and your ugly pointy nose and that….. that, pocket of yours. I better not see you hanging around here either or I'll fix you, if you know what I mean. There's no room around here for you, so get lost and, oh, if you're thinking of telling anyone what I said I will knock you into the next county. These antlers aren't here just for beautiful looks; I know how to use them. *(Bull E. moves his antlers around like he is really proud of them. Billy begins to "play possum". This act is achieved by rolling over, shutting his eyes, opening his mouth, and going limp. He slumps down and stares at the ground without moving. Bull E stands over Billy Bob with intimidating power.)* Do you hear me Billy Bob? Billy Bob *(Bull E gently pokes him with his stick and Billy Bob doesn't move.)* Freak! *(Bull E walks off, shaking his head. Felicia runs off. There is a pause here before Chapman comes on.)*

Chapman
(Chapman enters looking for Billy Bob.)
Billy Bob! Has anyone seen Billy Bob? *(The audience points to Billy Bob and Chapman rushes over.)* Billy are you all right, what happened? *(Billy is trying to get up off the ground).*

Billy Bob
Oh, Chapman?

Chapman
Billy Bob what happen to you, are you all right, did you fall down?

Billy Bob
I'm okay, I ah. *(Not knowing what to say because he is embarrassed)* I just slipped on some pine needles, that's all.

Chapman
Are you sure? I can go get Miss Deer.

Billy Bob
No, I'm fine, go ahead and get your backpack and we'll walk home. *(Watching him closely, Chapman walks off, Billy looks around and moves up to sit on the stump, frightened that Bully E might come back. He begins to cry)* Boy, why do I feel so bad? Well this day didn't turn out like I thought it would. I was so excited about coming to *(your)* school. Chapman made it sound like so much fun. But ever since I got here, I have been made fun of for being different and having different habits than the other animals. I don't know what to do. I'm afraid and embarrassed to tell my mom and make her worry. I could tell Miss Deer *(hesitate, sniffles as to cry)* but if she talks to Bull E, he'll really hurt me and everyone will call me a tattletale. I guess the best thing to do is not play ball, I don't feel like it anyway. Maybe it will be better if I just stay away. I wish I was back at my old school where there are more people like me.

Chapman
(From off stage Chapman yells,) Come on Billy, let's go! *(Billy Bob exits sadly)*

Scene 5

In the kitchen at Billy Bob's house, Billy enters from his day at school and Mama is waiting with his favorite cookies.

Mama O

Billy how was your first day at school? Was it as exciting as you thought it would be? Did you meet some interesting animals? Tell me all about it?

Billy Bob

Yes Mom, you could say that.

Mama O

Billy Bob, what's wrong?

Billy Bob

(Crossing his fingers so Mama can't see) Nothing Mom, I'm really tired. I played stickball after school and I have lots of homework to do. I just want to go to my room and get the work done.

Mama O

Okay sweetie, but if something was bothering you, you would tell me, right?

Billy Bob

Right Mom

Scene 6

Outside Billy Bob's house or use the playground scenery.

Felicia
Hey Chapman, wait up. I need to talk to you. *(looking at his sad face)* What's wrong?

Chapman
I just walked Billy Bob home; I don't think he's feeling well.

Felicia
That's why I want to talk to you. What did you see?

Chapman
I found him lying down at Pine Tree Park; he looked scared, sick or something. He said he slipped on the pine needles.

Felicia
Well, I don't think he's sick but I do know what's wrong.

Chapman
Really, what is it?

Felicia
Well, after we finished playing stickball, I went back to the park to get my glove and I sort of listened to Bull E Moose and Billy Bob talking.

Chapman
What did they say?

Felicia
Bull E was telling Billy not to come back to the team. I thought Billy Bob was ignoring him. He just sat down and closed his eyes and then Bull E finally went away.

Chapman
Oh Felicia, he wasn't ignoring him. Billy Bob was playing possum.

Felicia
Possum, what's that?

Chapman
Well when opossums are afraid, they pretend to be dead. They will even look like they are dead. They fall over and sometime stick out their tongues, even drool.

Felicia
Wow, I never heard of that.

Chapman
Yes, so Billy Bob must have been very upset and scared of what Bull E was saying. Should we tell someone? I don't know what to do, Felicia!

Felicia
Me either, if we tell, we will be tattle tales and I don't want to get into trouble or have Bull E start calling me names.

Chapman
Ya, you're right, Bull E will probably stop anyway, don't you think?

Felicia
Well maybe, but I'm confused. I'll see you tomorrow at school. *(They hang their heads and walk off in different directions.)*

Scene 7

*Cubby comes out with another sign that says, **The Next Morning**.*
Place: Pine Tree Park. The next day at stickball practice, all players are standing to the side talking. Chapman and Felicia come on and approach each other. Bull E is right stage, up against a tree tossing a ball and catching it with his glove.

Chapman
Hi Felicia, how are you feeling today?

Felicia
Hi Chapman, well I didn't sleep much last night, how about you?

Chapman
Me neither, I'm very upset about Billy Bob and still don't know what to do.

Bull E Moose
(From the other side of the stage) It's a rattlesnake! Oh no, rattlesnakes are invading us too!! He's going to bite me!! *(everyone is upset and running around the stage not knowing what to do)*

Felicia
Don't move Bull E. Miss Deer, Miss Deer!!!!

Bull E Moose
Help! Help! Someone help me!

Everyone
(All the characters are excited and upset and saying various things like "help, don't move", calling for the teacher. Have them run off stage)

Miss Dorrie Deer
(Running in hearing the excitement from the characters) Now children, be calm, what's going on? *(Everyone talks at once telling her about Bull E)* Calm down children. Let's think of a way to handle this. Don't move Bull E. Kids stay back!

Billy Bob
(Billy enters, sees the snake, grabs it and puts it in his pocket) What's going on?

Chapman
It's Bull E, he was cornered by that rattlesnake you put in your pouch, and he's wasn't moving so he wouldn't get bit.

Chapman
Billy, how did you do that? You are awesome! You saved Bull E's life! *(Bull E is looking embarrassed and is now holding his head down and slumped over, breathing heavily.)*

Billy Bob

Do what?

Felicia

You certainly don't deserve it after the mean things you've been saying about Billy Bob.

Bull E Moose

(Out of breath, very relieved in a really low voice) Ya well ah…

Felicia

Bull E, you should get down on your knees and beg Billy for forgiveness.

Chapman

Yes, Bull E, you haven't been very nice to Billy since he moved here.

Bull E Moose

Well, um, Billy I…..

Billy Bob

Bull E…..

Miss Dorrie Deer

(Interrupting the conversation) What is going on here? Billy, has something happened I should know about? *(Billy says nothing)* Children? *(She looks from Billy to the audience and back to Billy. Audience starts telling the teacher that Bull E was bullying Billy Bob. Encourage the audience to tell the story by saying, "What's going on kids, can anyone tell me what's going on? " Listens and then addresses Billy Bob)* I know you don't know us very well but I only want to help you. If something has happen, no matter how big or little, I'm sure we can work it out together.

Felicia

(Tugging on Miss Deer) Billy Bob saved Bull E Moose from the rattlesnake and I think Bull E should be grateful and apologize to Billy Bob.

Miss Dorrie Deer

Apologize? Don't you mean say thank you?

Chapman

No, Miss Deer, Bull E has been threatening Billy Bob since he came to school here and then Billy ran in and saved his live.

Billy Bob
(*Trying to interrupt*) But um...

Miss Dorrie Deer
Well Bull E is there any truth to this? *(waits for an answer that doesn't come.)* Children you should have come to me about this.

Chapman
We didn't want to tattle, Miss Deer.

Miss Dorrie Deer
Tattling? (*Turning to Bull E*) Did you say inappropriate things to Billy Bob?

Bull E Moose
Well, um, I didn't really mean it, it's just when Billy Bob came to school and everyone was paying attention to him and were watching his magic tricks, it made me mad that he got all the attention. I didn't like that, usually everyone is watching me play ball and telling me how good I am. So I thought if I told Billy not to try out for the team, he would get scared and go away. I didn't say it to hurt anyone.

Cubby
Bull E you're always bullying and teasing others. By the way, my name is Cubby, not Chubby! (*pause and looks at Miss Deer*) Miss Deer, he calls me names all the time.

Felicia
That's right Miss Deer, he did say mean things to Billy Bob, I heard it myself.

Chapman
Felicia and I talked about it yesterday. We really couldn't decide what to do. It was very confusing and made us feel really bad.

Miss Dorrie Deer
Well, okay, it's good that you are telling me this now. Bull E, I think it is best that you and I discuss this in private with your parents and the principal.

Bull E Moose
(*Hesitating*) I... um, yes Miss Deer.

Billy Bob
.. Chapman, Miss Deer, everyone..... listen to me. This is NOT a rattlesnake and I DIDN'T save his life! First of all this is an Eastern Milk Snake and even if it were a rattlesnake, opossums are immune to rattlesnake venom.

Bull E Moose
What!??

Billy Bob
...... that's right. If I get a rattlesnake bite, it won't hurt me. Opossums don't get sick from snakebites. We hunt rattlesnakes as part of our diet. Anyways I'm no hero; I was just hunting for something to eat.

Chapman
Oh yeah, that's right, don't you remember what Billy Bob said the first day of school, when he told the class about the habits of opossums? *(others shake their head agreeing)*

Miss Dorrie Deer
Nonetheless, this is something we need to discuss. Helping someone who hasn't been very kind is an act of good citizenship, whether the snake was poisonous or not. Billy Bob, would you like to tell me in your own words what happened?

Felicia
Go ahead Billy; you're safe with all of us here. Tell Miss Deer what happened at stickball the other day.

Billy Bob
Well, *(hesitates, looks around, at first he is afraid to talk, but starts out slowly, moves to center stage)* Bull E you did hurt my feelings *(pause)* and I felt like I didn't want to live here anymore. I didn't feel safe at school and wanted to stay home. I was very excited about moving here and meeting new friends. Although I met great new folks like Chapman, Cubby and Felicia, I still was scared to come to school. I thought I did something wrong. I didn't dare to tell anyone. I didn't want to be a tattletale either. I just didn't know what to do, so that's why I haven't been at stickball all week. I just figured ya'll wouldn't miss me and I could avoid being around Bull E.

Miss Dorrie Deer
Billy, remember that you can always go to a teacher, parents or an adult you trust for help. We are only looking out for your best interest! *(turns to all the animals)* And about the tattling, it's important to remember that if a person is getting hurt by a situation, then it is not tattling. *(Characters look at each other, surprised by this)*

Billy Bob
I didn't know that. I felt strange inside, it was a funny feeling I just couldn't figure it out. I thought I did something wrong.

Miss Deer
(Miss Deer gathers the animals together to talk with them, you can use this speech or have Miss Deer ask the students of ways to solve the problem, or use both, sometimes with younger children, some of the dialog will be too long to keep their attention,) Children, I know you are confused. Remember our talk at the stickball game? Being respectful and fair is the only way we can all get along.

Miss Deer

Accepting others for who they are helps us understand everyone's differences. We then find out that we're all not so different after all. You see, when we tease or bully someone, it creates bad feelings, not only to that person, but to others around them, the bystanders. It's okay to ask for help and a big step towards solving the problem. Ignoring or trying to handle it on your own can be harmful and sometime dangerous. *(Characters again look at Miss Deer with questioning expressions.)*

Felicia

Billy, I want to apologize to you.

Billy Bob

Why, Felicia? You didn't do anything.

Felicia

That's right, I didn't do anything! You see, Billy, I should have told someone what Bull E was doing sooner. I just ignored him hoping he would stop bullying. I didn't want to say anything because I was afraid he would tease me too. From now on, I will try to be a good citizen and ask an adult when someone needs help. No more bystanding for me, from now on you can count on me as, a …. STANDbyer, ya, that's it, a **STANDbyer!!**

Cubby

Me too, Billy Bob, I'll try hard to be a good friend to everyone.

Chapman

That goes for me too Billy Bob. *(speaks to the rest of the kids in the audience)* Well I don't know about you guys, but I'm really glad that Billy Bob migrated here. I've learned so much. It's important to respect and honor others for who they are. Now I understand what the school conduct means. We can learn a lot more by listening and respecting others.

Miss Deer

I know this is a great deal to think about. How about we set aside a time each week to talk about expected classroom behaviors and the way we want our school climate to be.

Cubby

Well, I know I want my "climate" to be warm and fuzzy!

Everyone

Yeah, okay, sounds good to me!

Miss Deer

Okay then, but in the meantime, if you have a question or problem……. *(Cubby cuts her off)*

Cubby

We'll come to you, Miss Deer! Now let's play some ball! *(the animals all yell, 'Yeah', and pick up their gloves and exit the stage.*

The End

Blocking Notes

Autographs

Sample Books from Bryson Taylor Publishing

Order Number	Product Description	Author-Illustrator	Price	Quantity	Total
6201	Sticks Stones and Stumped Children's Book	Deb Landry-Melissa Pelletier	$16.95		
6401	Yankee Go Home, Children's Book	Deb Landry-Christina St Cyr	$14.95		
6202	Sticks Stones and Stumped Play and Teacher Workbook	Landry	$29.95		
6203	Sticks Stones and Stumped Read A-long CD	Landry	$12.95		
6205	Sticks Stones and Stumped set book, CD, play	Landry	$54.95		
6210	CARE: Creating A Respectful Environment	The Students at Alfred Elementary School	$14.95		
6402	The Comfort Zone and Yankee Go Home Children's Play	D'Antona-Kevorkian-Landry	$24.95		
6409	Yankee Go Home Children's Audio Book Read Along CD	Landry	$12.95		
6410	One Bad Thing	John Goff	$10.95		
6300	A Bully Grows Up: Erik Meets the Wizard Student Book	Caryn Sabes Hacker	$12.95		
6301	A Bully Grows Up: Erik Meets the Wizard Adult Guide	Caryn Sabes Hacker	$15.95		
6302	A Bully Grows Up: Erik Meets the Wizard Audio Book	Caryn Sabes Hacker	$12.95		
6501	101 Facts about Bullying: What Everyone Should Know	Kevorkian-D'Antona	$32.95		

Get your copy of *Sticks Stones and Stumped* at brysontaylorpublishing.com and Visit our site for a complete catalog of safe school and bullying prevention publications

Bryson Taylor Publishing

*Creating a Respectful Environment
One Book at a Time*

About the Author

Deb Landry is the author of the best selling children's book, *Sticks Stones and Stumped, Yankee Go Home, and the* co-author of *The Comfort Zone* with Meline Kevorkian Ed.D., and Robin D'Antona, Ed.D. She is a freelance writer and a parenting coach specializing in social awareness behaviors and character education and has authored several interactive children's mentoring plays. She a member of the team that authored the Maine State Best Practices in Bullying and Harassment Prevention Manual.

Landry is the co-founder, President/CEO and former Executive Director of Crossroads Youth Center, a nonprofit performing art based afterschool program and is a facilitator for *Real Life — Real Talk™*.

She passionately shares her expertise through lectures, workshops, books, author visits, keynote speaking and her parent coaching practice. With recognition and several awards for her work with children, Landry has been interviewed and featured on NBC, CBS, national radio, and several publications including *Raising Maine Magazine, Seventeen, Women's Day, GABonline and Child Magazine.*

Her new book, *The Snapdragon Princess,* with Kim Parrish is due out August 2009.

Deb Landry may be contacted through her website at:
deblandry.com brysontaylorpublishing.com or on her blog at raisingmaine.com/heartstrings.

Bryson Taylor Publishing
199 New County Road
Saco, Maine 04072
www.brysontaylorpublishing.com
207-838-2146

www.ingramcontent.com/pod-product-compliance
Lightning Source LLC
Chambersburg PA
CBHW081219230426
43666CB00015B/2799